The pig pen had ten pigs in it.
The big fat pig is the mum.

A pig did not get fed. It hid in the pig pen.

Meg's dad got the vet.
The vet said, 'It is not fit.'
Meg said, 'It is sad.'

The vet said, 'Give him to Meg.'
'The pig is Meg's pet,' Dad said.

Meg fed him.
'The pig got fat,' Meg said.

Meg got him fit.
'The pig can dig,' Meg said.

Meg got him a bed.

'The pig naps in it,' Meg said.

Dad said, ‘Meg, the pig is a tip-top pet!’

The Blue Jackal

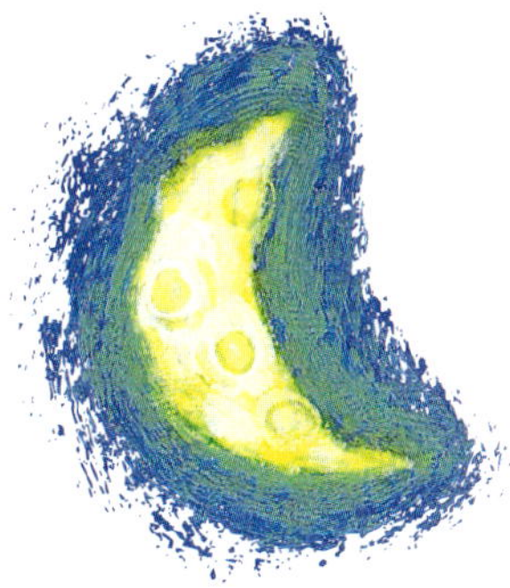

written by Jenny Alexander
illustrated by Stephen Waterhouse

Long ago in India, there was a jackal.

He lived in a forest with all his jackal friends.

One evening he wandered into the town.

He fell into a tub of blue dye, and he could not get out.
So he had to swim in the dye all night.

In the morning, a man came and pulled him out.

He thought the jackal was dead.

But the jackal was just pretending.

“What has happened to you?”
the other jackals asked.

The blue jackal said, “The goddess of the forest made me blue.”

"Blue is the colour of kings, and now I am king of all the animals."

The jackals bowed low, with their ears to the ground.

And the blue jackal became their king.

Soon the other animals heard about the new king.

They all bowed low, even the lions and tigers.

The blue jackal said, “I have lions and tigers for friends now …

… I do not want you jackals for friends any more."

The jackals were angry.
But the oldest one had an idea.

"The lions and tigers have not noticed that their king is a jackal," he said.

“But if we howl at dusk, he will howl back, because that is what jackals do.”

So the jackals howled at dusk,
and the blue jackal howled back.

"Our king is just a jackal!"
cried the lions and tigers.

"We eat jackals!"

So the jackal who did not
want jackals for friends ended up
having no friends at all!